Challenging the Devil's Narrative

Challenging the Devil's Narrative

Poems and Rhymes to Explain the Times

by
LEE WILLIAM JONES

RESOURCE *Publications* · Eugene, Oregon

CHALLENGING THE DEVIL'S NARRATIVE
Poems and Rhymes to Explain the Times

Resource Publications
An Imprint of Wipf and Stock Publishers
199 W. 8th Ave., Suite 3
Eugene, OR 97401

www.wipfandstock.com

PAPERBACK ISBN: 979-8-3852-6757-6
HARDCOVER ISBN: 979-8-3852-6758-3
EBOOK ISBN: 979-8-3852-6759-0

VERSION NUMBER 010226

Contents

Challenging the Devil's Narrative Explained

(breaking down common preconceptions that can be barriers to God and Christianity)

The devil's overall narrative (which incorporates many aspects) is the devil's most potent and effective weapon (through influencing people's thought processes), using mass media for example, he uses twisted reason (making the straight path crooked) to validate not connecting with Christianity as a religion and therefore leaving a person powerless against his actions, using the regular narrative such as "organized religions are a man made construct to control people and make money" for example. Yet, Christianity did not start as an organized construct it grew from nothing as people could recognize God and the truth within the teachings, Christianity started as one man speaking wisdom and truth then grew on merit, its central goal has never been money, if it was then it would have been so from the beginning with a set financial business model at its central core and the desired outcome of wealth for its organizers. Indeed, Jesus and the twelve disciples had nothing yet could have easily used their influence to become very rich men. Although, within any group of people there will always be a bad apple (that can be corrupted) moving forward, Judas as an early example.

Moreover, if control means guiding people to good then surely that is a positive aspect, indeed isn't that what the laws of every land aims to do, guide us from bad behavior to good behavior, if we rejected national laws on the basis of 'controlling behaviors' then there would be anarchy, the devil's favored outcome? The irony and contradiction is that many people who reject Christianity based on an 'organized controlling religion' very much value living in a society controlled through law and order. This is the nuance of the devil's overall narrative that sounds reasonable on the surface yet makes little logical sense under further inspection, the truth (God) will always make sense at some level, the lie (devil) will always be a contradiction, as it contradicts the truth.

The devil's Narrative: (short version)

An investigation into the devil's motivation, a written account of connected events to explain his intention. Good is bad and bad is good the devil's character is understood, he's at war, you may not know it, he'll tempt your soul but he'll never show it, subtle and devious it's hard to stop it, upside down, inside out, and back to front, he'll confuse and tempt on the devil's hunt, what is right and what is wrong in the devil's disorder your singing his song, the central director the soul collector, he's got an army because he's at war, your soul is his target rich or poor, manipulating your thoughts and your actions, if he revealed himself there would be comprehension which would undermine his own intention, he's not stupid I forgot to mention, using the media and his minions for misdirection, making bad popular and good an abomination, bringing you low so you act out of anger, hate and desperation, making it even worse by calling you to intoxication to deal with your own situation, with even more control over you through your addiction, the devil's affliction, the devil's playground he knows what he is doing, the devil's playground your soul he's pursuing, he's seen it all before it's nothing new he knows what works and what to do, the devils target, the target is you.

Wise words

Fear of God is wisdom, wisdom leads to understanding, understanding to knowledge and knowledge is power.

Why write this book of poetry?

Knowledge is power, when a person has more understanding they are greater equipped to resist manipulation, similar to watching a magic trick but knowing how it is achieved, knowledge, it is more difficult to be misled when you have a general understanding of the overall process. Involvement (whether you like it or not) in a war that you are unaware of leaves a person underprepared and vulnerable, comparable to having an enemy backbiting you, but you do not know it is happening, or who, yet you feel the effects, but you can't quite put your finger on why and where. Highlighting the devil's narrative firstly explains that we are in a war for our souls raged by the devil, the best way for the devil to win this war for souls is to keep people generally ignorant not only of the existence of the devil but also his goals through a certain overall narrative.

A crucial part of the devil's narrative is to engender doubt which puts in place barriers to Christianity, as Christianity is the only power over the devil (which is the last thing he wants), directing people away from Christianity leaves them powerless against the devil's actions and temptations, doubt such as, does the devil exist or even does God exist, for example? If either God or the devil revealed themselves this would take away free will based on faith as we would know that both competing sides exist, a war, yet not based on our own search, character and personal journey of discovery, similar to writing an exam but already given the answers, the test then becomes irrelevant and worthless as a measure, free will measures wisdom, understanding and character. This book aims to provide the reader with reasoned knowledge and understanding using common sense information (the truth will always make sense at some level) to greater prepare a person, young or old, for the life journey ahead and beyond.

Why Use Poetry to Convey A Message?

Poetry is a great way to encapsulate knowledge in a quick and easy to read format. Not all poetry is used for expressing emotions, exploring the beauty and wonder in the world and storytelling, poetry is also a great way to share unique ideas in a short and easy flowing format. As a youth the assumption was that traditional poetry was only really ever used in an arty context by artists expressing existential narratives inside somewhat restrictive poetic structures only for the preserve of the sensitive and emotionally connected within a largely academic arena. However, utilizing the strengths of poems within a prose poem format as almost a synopsis of what can be complex subject matters avoids having to write long winded and complex dissertations that could easily lose the reader along the way. Poems summarize in an easy-to-read shorter context to more easily engage the reader that no other form of writing can achieve due to its simplicity of having to condense vast amounts of knowledge into a brief and flowing arrangement.

Modern Poetry

Poetry in motion that requires a devotion taking complex subjects breaking them down to a rapid rendition a beginning middle and an end with a concise conclusion to avoid any confusion, time is your enemy not your best friend, talking with a rhyme and a flow to allow the message to follow, in a world of social media where the attention span is minimal if it's not rapid and snappy it makes it invisible, when you write a dissertation to explain a situation you risk losing attention and participation as the reader loses interest throughout the duration, informative, quick, short and for the reader easy, modern poetry for the 21st century.

Creation: God's Perfection

Look and see, pause a while take it all in, look at the basics that's where to begin, what we take for granted is where the answers lay a design so profound yet seen every day, it's always been there it's nothing special yet look at the detail at the sea and the air, the moon and the sun now you are seeking your journey has begun. Millions of combined interconnections all working as one to create a perfect perfection from the animals, insects, the birds to the bees, the air that we breath to the trees and the seas, recycling fresh water for us to thrive, with fertile ground and animals acceptable to eat so we can survive, the moon just the right distance and size to control the tide, we're not too close or far from the sun the perfect location, with a magnetic field to protect from the sun's radiation, there's millions of moving parts working in complete and perfect collaboration.

Show me the evidence and I will change my position, but when I look at the earth I see a perfect design and the perfect creation, who could look at the evidence of the wonder of the earth and see another explanation, watching TV as reality when it states quite clearly this is for entertainment purposes only, not to mention the forces of gravity, only the fool would assume this all happened accidently, hope and fantasy colliding with reality, nothing can come from nothing when calculated mathematically, the only planet with recognized life, millions of accidents working in harmony, how can this be, it defies the laws of probability all working together so complete and concisely.

We look into the stars for billions of light years, back to the beginning of time, yet nothing is found, no signs of life not a word not a sound, there's nothing out there in space and time no evidence of life not a word not a sign, if life happened once then it will happen again and again, over time, with billions of years of universe development, yet you gaze at the earth and declare it an accident, and you say you're intelligent, then when nothing is found your position moves coming up with far away theories of life that can't be proved, with all that is said what ever happened to evidence led, as you look in despair with a burning hope and desire clouding your effectiveness whilst not accepting the evidence, that is here tangible and can be seen, as you hope beyond hope clinging onto a dream.

Why does it matter if God exists or Not?

There is a right way and a wrong way, a path to follow, the wrong way is broad and the right way narrow, when there is no distinction between the two, right and wrong all becomes true, the truth must be separate from the lie, right must be separate from wrong, the moral from the immoral, if there's confusion which path do we follow, but with God we have to pick a side the good or the bad we decide, God is good which makes the other side bad now we've got a choice the decisions are hard, a moral dilemma, which way do we go now there's a choice to be made do we choose right or do we choose wrong and can you be swayed, God exists for our salvation to guide us in the right direction, to avoid destruction, he draws the line between right and wrong, the dark and the light in the moral fight, ever present but out of sight.

Does the devil Exist?

Where there is hate, jealousy, deception and greed, there he is, where there is lust, distrust, backbiting and persecution, there he is, you know his work but still you dismiss, the central controller we are all on his list, the origin of darkness it's hard to resist, sowing the seeds of negativity on fertile ground using people's naivety, his secret weapon is anonymity relying on people's gullibility, you know his work yet you cannot see, an undercover force the worst sort of enemy, out of sight is out of mind with anonymity making his targets blind, if you don't know there's an army at war for your soul it's easier for the devil to deceive and control, to catch you underprepared, weak and scared, attacked from all sides as he crawls and slithers strikes and hides, he knows your weakness as he creeps and spies, where there is the devil there is his lies, to avoid your demise, you'd better get wise.

Theory of Evolution Causing Confusion

A child like theory that most could conceive with no conclusive evidence yet still they believe, it's called a theory because it lacks reality, coming up with the theory first then trying to develop the evidence to try to support the ideology, evolving, yet you confuse the question that we are solving. I came with an open mind but all I can do is to look and to find. If fishes moved from the sea to land to develop into a human state, then how have we all evolved at exactly the same rate?

If fishes move from sea to land it will be on multiple occasions over the centuries, Millenia and generations, meaning different human descendants at differing times and stages so when you walk down the street you should see people at different stages of their evolutionary change, from later to earlier a different and wide evolutionary range, within their specific evolutionary stage, with some humans even more advanced than us today depending on their evolutionary age, depending on when their evolutionary fish decided to move from sea to land over millions of years and centuries yet all we see is every human with the same evolutionary identity.

It's impossible for fishes to come out of the sea at one specific time frame as evolution would continue again and again, even to this day, yes of course all earth dwelling life will have similar DNA, if evolution was true it would be all around us for all to see, evolving, living and breathing in our community, there would be no need for selective, obscure and ambiguous evidence if evolution was actually real and in existence, as it would be all around us as an ongoing process.

"Quick scramble let's make up some counter theory, there's got to be an angle, there's got to be, it's something we got to do, I'm not letting this theory go after all I've been through, but how can evolution suddenly stop or be at a certain time just because we want it to, evolution would be a varied and multiple ongoing process, even primates coming down from the trees and then walking upright would continue, this is true, give me some time I'll have to think this one through, but I'm sure we can come up with something we'll rearrange and make do, we'll find some evidence we can change and construe, wait, I'll look and see, remember, I'm a professor, they think I'm intelligent, they'll listen to me".

The devil's Narrative: (long version)

An investigation into the devil's motivation, a written account of connected events to explain the devil's intention, connecting his character to his narrative to allow for interpretation, know your enemy to provide some protection, free reign to roam the world to influence people through affliction, jealousy, lust, and a love of money as a temptation, are these situations just a coincidence or the devil's intention, is it just chance or his intervention, is it a one off or a continuation, if it's persistent then that usually means you've got the devil's attention, you know what to do in that situation, go to God for your salvation, through Jesus Christ without hesitation.

Good is bad and bad is good the devil's character is understood, he's at war, you may not know it, he'll tempt your soul but he'll never show it, subtle and devious it's hard to stop it, good is bad and bad is good the devil's narrative he's up to no good, upside down, inside out, and back to front he'll confuse and tempt on the devil's hunt, which direction do you go with the devil's confusion it's hard to know, what is right and what is wrong in the devil's disorder your singing his song, the central director the soul collector, he's got an army because he's at war, your soul is his target rich or poor.

The devil can't directly physically hurt you, God has set this boundary, but he can control situations directing your free will through manipulation giving opportunity by providing temptation guiding you in his own direction, manipulating your thoughts and your actions, the devil hides to avoid attention, if he revealed himself there would be comprehension which would undermine his own intention, he's not stupid I forgot to mention, if you don't understand him and his calculations then you make yourself ripe for manipulation, using the media and his minions for misdirection, making bad popular and good an abomination, if it looks good but is bad then it is his narration, bringing you low so you act out of anger, hate and desperation, making it even worse by calling you to intoxication to deal with your own situation, with even more control over you through your addiction, the devil's affliction, the devil's playground he knows what he is doing, the devil's playground your soul he's pursuing, he's seen it all before it's nothing new he knows what works and what to do, the devils target, the target is you.

Desperation: The Human Condition

Hello God, are you there? I've been praying so hard but you don't seem to care. God are you there? I seem to have a faulty connection in need of repair. God are you there? I'm in pain and despair, this pain is more than I can bear. God are you there? I'm being destroyed, I've been calling you so much you must be annoyed. God are you there? I'm down on my knees; I'm begging you please. God are you there?...

God's Silence

Free will must be free, if God revealed himself then my decisions are guided by this knowledge and not by me, think of talking to God as a counselling session, he's not there to give advice, he's there to listen, for honest expression, yet is he really silent when the bible has been provided, his guidelines have been noted, written and decided, the voice of God is there if you listen informing our actions and every decision, it's no coincidence that the bible is the world's most prolific book but it's then up to you if you want to read and to look, free will, it must be so, where are we now and where do we go, guidance is provided for the seeds that we sow, through his writing he's a God we can know, we can hear his voice inwardly through thoughts and dreams, when you know God's character you know that it's him, because when it's the devil he'll guide you to sin, we can see him through his works, he's nowhere yet everywhere, still it says in the bible he can hear us through prayer, if you're looking for God then look for him there, when you open the bible the silence is broken with all the words that he has spoken, even Job had his troubles to bear as he called out to God yet found him nowhere, his test of faith with all the pain he received even so still he believed, yet, when you call out to God it must be true, because if you've denied him, then he'll deny you.

God as a Fantasy Being

Experiencing the realities of earth is like using my car, I have never met or spoken to the creator and designer, but I know their work, therefore I know they exist somewhere, out there, their work confirms their reality, I don't assume that just because I have never met my car's creator and designer that they are then somehow a fantasy, how silly would I be if I looked at my car and assumed that it happened accidently, silly me.

The Human Condition Never Changes

Progression through technology and society, yet regression through philosophy, words written over 2000 years ago have no relevance to now, yet the human condition never changes throughout the ages, good versus evil that age old fight, wrong or right, do we choose darkness or do we choose light, we are born, age and die, we try to tell the truth yet sometimes we lie, we all experience love, hate, loss, conflict and redemption it's always been the same throughout all human civilization, trying to balance the ethical dimension, what's right or wrong the moral decision, we aspire to be good but fall short on many occasions, navigating relationships and human emotions, sometimes we succeed and sometimes we fail we can all tell a very similar tale, in the future we can all even be in a full size life like computer simulation but will still face the same moral situations, tempted by temptation, greed and need, hope and desperation, the human condition, the same now as it was then, the same rendition, over and over again, a different time yet the same, and always will be, the human condition that never changes throughout all of history and into eternity.

The Gray Area

The devil uses his lies with a mixture of truth to form a disguise, when truth and lies are intertwined the truth and the lie can't be defined, everything becomes a gray area, no wrong or right with the darkness mixed in to dim the light as the line between good and bad fades from sight, right or wrong must be distinct, if the line between right and wrong is blurred then this can change the way people think, the gray area that can justify bad intention through ensuring confusion, open to a multitude of different interpretations depending on intentions, the truth can be stretched to the limit before you know it there's no truth in it, with free will and truth effected as a person's behavior can be manipulated with any decision selected, the gray area is the devil's play area, validating immoral action and manipulation by leaving the truth open to interpretation.

If God exists why do bad things happen?

The devil is bad yet must be here as the free choice option, good or bad it's our decision, when people question "if God exists then why do bad things happen?", the devil has to be here as an opposing opinion, and with him comes jealousy, hate and manipulation with bad intention, good and bad in competition, yet people are free to choose their own words and actions, for clarification, people do the things that are bad, it's their free choice, it's people not God.

Why does the devil exist?

The devil exists as a force to resist, it all comes down to free choice, which do we choose, is it good or bad do we win or lose, without the devil there would only be one voice taking away our freedom of choice, right or wrong without the devil the choice would be gone, good and bad must have a division, because if right and wrong are the same then where's the decision, with the seeds that we sow without free choice, are we good or bad, how will God know, the devil is bad and God is good, now free will has opposing options and is well understood.

The Gift of Time

Time taken for granted yet is more precious than gold, when it is running out added time can't be bought or be sold, time only goes forward and never backwards, you can spend your time but you can't buy more of it, you can waste your time but you can't replace it, in bad times it drags and in good times it's rapid, use your time wisely as it's in short supply seems abundant in the beginning but can end in a blink of an eye, God knows when it's your time to die, your time is yours, a perfect gift, so don't let it decay, do what makes you content and happy without any delay, today's the day, don't hesitate or it will slip away, your time has a beginning and an end, time can be your enemy or your best friend, the wise person thinks of their death because it reminds them that time is finite it's what you do with it that matters it's never too late, don't wait for that time when you're older when you feel the ticking of time much closer and you start thinking about the time you have left, then time becomes valuable, make time valuable now, get in first before it's too late while you're young enough to alter your fate, incline your ear to the ticking of the clock, because when you die, the ticking stops.

Scientific

Science does not prove that God does not exist it proves that he exists, when we look into detail into what God has created it tells us more about how it was invented, the details revealed, in the original vacuum of space where nothing was there no elements not even air, how did all the exact required elements that were never previously there appear in one place from the vacuum of space to create the big bang for the planets formulation, and who constructed the explosion taking us from nothing to our universal planetary progression with earth as the supreme ideal destination, the exact chemical mixture and quantity in one location then ignited, which can't be an accidental realistic reality within the laws of probability without an intervention and an overall strategy to initiate the universe with all its complexity.

God as the pre-existing law and energy directing consciously in just one attempt then created perfectly, if you say that because earth exists this is a 100% probability this does not say if it happened accidentally, with the precise universal precision for life and chemistry calculated exactly, if earth is just a coincidence and happened randomly then in our universe earth and life should appear repeatedly.

Thanks to science the hand of God has been clarified and identified, as any scientist will tell you any experimental activity must first be planned in detail to ensure its validity and overall accuracy, it's not God verses science it's God and science as an alliance, God is the ultimate scientist giving us earth the ultimate gift.

Know thy enemy

Knowledge of the enemy is the best defense against wickedness that leads to distress, you may not know you're in a war but be assured that the devil is out there keeping score, understand his character then you'll know when he is on the attack using his demons behind your back, in the background pulling the strings when he bites and strikes the devil stings, he will use your weakness and previous sins against you, understand your enemy that's what you must do, know thy enemy because he knows you.

Money or Greed

We all need money for our basic survival, yet love of money is the root of all evil, camel and needle come to mind as when we have more than we need and don't use the rest to help the less fortunate then this is greed, greed is a need indeed, the enemy of equality that blinds us to other people's humanity, as greed can be an incurable disease because all it wants to do is to please by serving our every insatiable need, yet money and power are also connected to a person's sense of pride and superiority the devil's personality, money that props up an inflated sense of confidence and dignity not based on morality but based on money, because of money they're all quick to agree, that adulation don't come for free, without your money where would you be because when the money's gone all this will flee, with all the friends that money can buy, yet the poor and needy you're quick to deny.

Gratitude

Gratitude develops the right attitude, thanksgiving is effective as it provides perspective, it's easy for the devil to pile so much pressure on that we forget what we have and only focus on what's wrong, don't sing his song through negativity always look at what you have with positivity, it's your choice, you can either count your blessings or succumb to the devil's voice, constantly whispering in your ear about how bad things are focusing on your pain and fear, before the tears, remember gratitude, remind yourself of all you have that is good, don't get your situation misunderstood, we all have positive aspects to our life even in the most dire of situations, gratitude provides hope by changing a negative interpretation into appreciation.

Humility

We are all God's creation none better or worse, even the bad one's can change their course, repent and convert, humility is something that needs to be engrained and observed, is easy to get proud but the fall is hard when the bubble bursts, don't get too high and don't get too low whether you win or lose greet with a bow, humility a vital tool in the stresses and strains of modern society, the opportunity of clarity free of insanity the most precious of gifts with pride as your enemy, to sum up with some simplicity throughout your life journey living in humility ensures your stability.

Hope versus Desperation

The human body can be broke then repaired, yet a broken spirit leads to despair, as the devil grinds you down a broken spirit is the devil's goal because when we're broken we're more easy for the devil to control, influencing us in the wrong direction in any situation exploiting a person's pain, fear and desperation, hope is the promise of a better tomorrow even though today may be engulfed in sorrow, who can fix a broken spirit, God is hope through faith you may not know it, trust in the Lord and he'll get you through it, the best way to heal a broken spirit, free from manipulation, his strength provides healing inspiration, what's broke can be healed for your salvation based on a firm foundation that never falters or changes in any situation, yet in the absence of hope there's desperation.

UFO: Why Put on a Show?

This is a surprising development, how can the popularity of UFO's aid in the devil's malevolence? The gray area that cannot be proved or disproved yet taken for granted, that fits right in with the devil's character, motives, and narrative, UFO's putting on obvious shows is there something that someone wants us to know? UFO's are a popular assertion, yet if there's life on other planets then this undermines God's universal creation and the uniqueness of humans as his invention, UFO's a malevolent intervention that just so happens to align with the devil's intentions, who also has the power to create these situations, free to roam the earth to create confusion, when through extensive scientific observation no signs of other life outside of earth can be found in any other location, if life is elsewhere and all around then there's not one God others can be found, or even that life accidently evolved, if you're questioning if there is a God then with the devil involved your question is solved.

Ghosts

The Holy Ghost and Jesus' resurrection are two unique situations, yet if anyone can come back from the dead this undermines Jesus' unique power over death, that he sacrificed himself to pay our debt, if random ghosts are a dime a dozen it dilutes the fact that Jesus had risen, the devil's mission, to avoid any confusion ghosts are demons through impersonation as the dead are dead and in another location, if you think ghosts are spirits of the dead and that we can all come back here after death then this reduces the value of life and enhances communication leaving you open to the devil's manipulation through direct conversations, Ouija boards and seance sessions, never talk to a demon as they are smarter than you, as they will then influence you to do what they want you to do, yet free will is here so you're free to choose your own destination all Christianity can do is try to point you in a positive direction, you can know if it's true as Christianity wants the best for you, something the devil will never do, the devil's illusions undermining God and Jesus through his intrusions, ghosts are the devil's invention causing fear and anxiety as his intention, aligned with the devil's character and his motivation to undermine God and Jesus to avoid your salvation.

What happens when we die?

All the information is available just look in the bible, or look at other options to see which one is feasible as our decisions are our own and individual, the forest that hides the tree, which one is true which to believe, put in the effort to search and you will receive, if there was only Christianity available you'd have no need to choose, right or wrong, do you win or lose, choose a religion or reject it all, in the end do we stand or do we fall, this is on you, what will you do, as there is no middle ground if you search with an open mind the answer can be confirmed and found, you decide, yet when you make a decision to choose nothing don't be misled as the undecided are already dead, are you rotten or redeemable, is your transition possible, do you make excuses or are you accountable, free choice, our actions decide our consequences, find wisdom, hold on to truth and compassion to gain life everlasting, what happens when we die, what happens on the other side, put quite simply, you decide.

Fear

It's never been love and hate it's always been love and fear, when you conquer fear love can draw near, fear is our biggest weakness and the devil's greatest weapon against us, yet when fear is stored safe from exploitation we can live life without restriction, regret and hesitation, placing our fear in God leaves it in a safe place so it cannot be used for manipulation then we can move forward and fulfil our potential, put fear into God's hands then continue on with your dreams, aspirations and plans, don't let fear stop you, do what you got to do, try something new, in the absence of fear your dreams can come true.

Wisdom

Seek wisdom first to provide understanding, fear of the Lord is a good place for starting, finding wisdom can be a difficult task but all you need to do is to ask, follow her path to avoid any shame, even when doing the right thing usually means short term pain but in the end it's you who will gain, as the fool and the wise are not the same, events will happen to both but wisdom and foolishness will decide our reactions guiding each person in different directions, some to contentment and some to destruction, wisdom is based on knowing right from wrong, truth and compassion that leads to understanding and understanding to knowledge then knowledge to action, a spiritual purpose bringing order to chaos, that provides you peace by making sense out of confusion and nonsense, to avoid the stresses and bitterness with a content long life as a natural consequence.

Futility of Life

Futility like grasping for the wind, chasing riches that most will never find, in the place of justice wickedness was found, you sort wisdom but only became more foolish, you sort joy but in the end it only brought you sorrow, you rejoiced in your labor but then only saw futility, you sort honor and gain and even fame, you were nice to the right people playing the game with money your aim, then eventually you look back and what do see, only futility.

Discover the ultimate purpose for filling the void, if we want a content life, this we cannot avoid. Yes, it's all in vain if you labor and toil for yourself and your own but ignore those unknown, give to charity, this can be time, possessions or money, the more you give to charity the less your life lives in vanity, give a little or give a lot it all depends on what you have got, give whatever you can afford it all has the same reward, as who is there to testify when you die what will they say on that day, when all you take with you is that which you have given away, stored in heaven where it will never decay.

Look and see there's your legacy, the multitude that you helped are there as your testimony recorded in eternity some may be known and some in anonymity, yet don't seek publicity or your reward will fade into obscurity, charity will remain to validate your existence and honor your name more important than success, profit or fame, make giving your aim, the more you give the more you gain, then my friend your life was never in vain, so let it be said with some humility that only charity is the victor of futility.

God's Wrath Done out of Love

What does God's wrath mean to you who may not have experienced it, what does it mean to the untouched, their just words or a phrase, but once you have been touched by his wrath it will alter your ways, sing his praise, you're a new person now, with fear of the Lord, then at once all fears are replaced with all your fear now stored in a safe place, so any fear of the devil and his games can be ignored, when you have felt God's wrath for goodness you know for sure the truth of his word and the strength of his sword, in an effort to get you wise and fear the Lord.

The only way to change and gain is through pain, but don't go insane, he's a God of infinite mercy so confess your sins and he will listen, whatever you have done can be forgiven, as the devil wants you, it's never too late, the devil tells you that God does not exist as he wants your soul to go on his list, that's how precious you are, opportunity missed.

Yet find the strength to rejoice although his wrath is mighty and stern, be wise as he's doing it so we can learn, if he didn't care he'd have no concern, God's wrath is done for correction the devil's hate is done for destruction, it's natural to take correction as a violation and say "if there was a God this pain wouldn't happen", but don't be fooled or think it rejection just as a parent chastises to direct their child in the right direction.

Remember we're all special and precious and he wants us to win, yet the gate is narrow, endure in his wrath, get wise, and depart from your sin, it takes effort to correct us, yet it's all for a purpose, there's a war for your soul so take the push with the shove to earn a place in heaven above, endure and change in his wrath, as he's doing it for you, it's done out of love.

Why does God love and forgive us all?

Why does God forgive us so much throughout our lives, it's easy for us to love him but why does he love us with all our sin? Heaven and hell are separate situations but on earth these two variations are in the same location, open to hope but also desperation, with the devil free to roam the earth to cause pain and confusion, so where there is love there is also manipulation, where there is peace there is also temptation, God knows the power of the devil which is why he cast him out of heaven, so hate and love can have a separation, so in heaven love can be pure without fear as a poison, if the devil can cause so much concern in heaven with the best of the best, with the angels who know that God exists, then how much more difficult is it for us to live with the devil, survive and resist, the ultimate test, so why does God love us so much and constantly forgive, because he knows full well the place where we live.

Experiences That Lead to Knowledge

My experiences are my own, I will not tell you what I have heard or seen in an effort to try to condone, or sway your view in an attempt to say what you should or should not do, whatever you should do is up to you, you don't need to know what anyone else has gone through, as what's happened to me might be different for you.

My experiences are mine they're not yours as we all have different characters, weakness and flaws for the devil to exploit and reveal yet our experiences are individual, unique and real, we can be supported, but we're on our spiritual journey alone that's part of the deal.

I won't tell you my experiences year after year that have brought me here, just know that the devil and his demons are present and near, the devil is my Lord's footstool this has been made very clear, so I have no fear, you have to have your own individual, unique experiences to adapt and grow, my experiences have shown me that the devil is a conquered foe, from my own personal experiences, that's all that I think that I want you to know.

Bonus section: common sayings explored

A slight break from poetry now yet still aligned with the overall ethos of this book which is to challenge the devil's overall narrative through utilizing the power of words. In many moral dilemma circumstances certain well-known phrases and sayings are regularly used to validate unethical decisions in one common and easily accessible catchphrase. The devil's narrative is subtle and comes in many forms, the use of popular catchphrases is a common tool for the devil to validate and condone certain behaviors and actions.

The devil's influence in theses well-known sayings is evidenced as the behaviors and actions promoted supports negativity and immorality (in-line with the devil's character), yet on the surface appear reasonable, demonstrating the subtlety of the devil making use of clever and indirect methods to achieve a desired outcome. Nonetheless, these sayings are so imbedded into many societies without challenge that they then become an accepted truth, yet very difficult to challenge due to their fluidity and simplicity of use within sentences and conversations. In order to effectively challenge the devil's overall narrative, in this instance through common catchphrases, the challenge must be as popular and fluid as the catchphrase, but first we need to know which certain common catchphrases may be misleading and why.

Here are some examples:

"Charity begins at home"

The proverb 'charity begins at home' was popularized by Sir Thomas Browne in his 1642 work *Religio Medici* (*The Religion of a*

Physician). This well-known saying is usually associated as coming from the bible so coming with an authentic ethical background, however no such saying was ever mentioned in the bible, for good reason. The saying 'charity begins at home' validates selfishness and keeping wealth between a person and their own whereas charity is about helping people in need whether we know them or not. Indeed, helping yourself and your own is what demons are allowed to do which might tell you how this random saying promotes anything other than Christian actions leading to the selfish hoarding of wealth and assistance. Indeed, in this 'charity begins at home' scenario the good Samaritan would not exist as a precedent as he assisted a person in need that he did not know.

"Good guys always come last"

'Good guys always come last' originates from a 1946 remark by baseball manager Leo Durocher about the New York Giants, yet has somehow become a well-known catch phrase around the world promoting unscrupulous behavior in order to achieve success. 'Good guys always come last' quite clearly promotes being devious and in essence bad in order not to come last and/or constantly lose, this well-known saying then promotes changing a person's behavior from good to bad in order to achieve success in any given circumstance, validating unethical conduct.

However, when this well-known catchphrase is critically analyzed the idea that good guys always come last is incongruent to winning as winning through ethical conduct can make any victory a total win, yet further creates a win-win situation for the person because losing also means winning, as you may have lost but with your ethics and good reputation intact a priceless element which ironically enhances your chances of success as to be recognized as a bad person (immoral) can only diminish a person's career prospects (as employers do not generally want immoral people) and ongoing personal relationships. A safety net win-win situation for the ethical as being bad (unethical) and also losing means you have a lose-lose total loss situation where you may have sacrificed your good reputation yet also lost, even if the bad person wins, they may win the given circumstance yet lose their good reputation so can never be a total win. However, winning and maintaining your ethics creates a total win with a safety net reputation win meaning that you can never totally lose being a good person. In essence then good guys actually will always win at some level, yet, a bad person will always lose at some level, even when they win.

www.ingramcontent.com/pod-product-compliance
Lightning Source LLC
Chambersburg PA
CBHW060627030426
42337CB00018B/3230